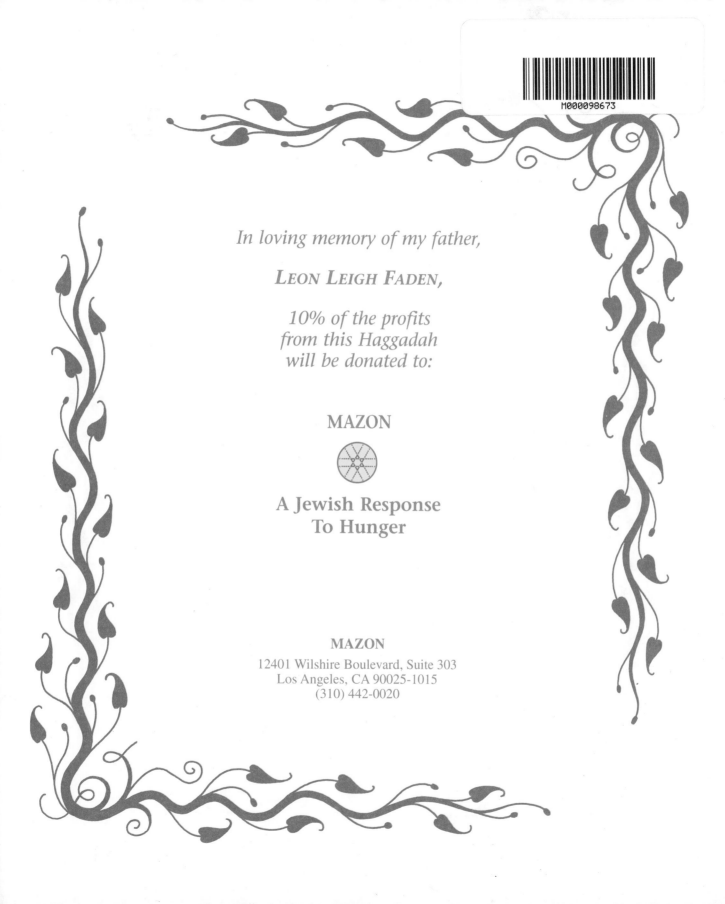

In loving memory of my father,

LEON LEIGH FADEN,

10% of the profits
from this Haggadah
will be donated to:

MAZON

A Jewish Response
To Hunger

MAZON
12401 Wilshire Boulevard, Suite 303
Los Angeles, CA 90025-1015
(310) 442-0020

How Precious Your Loving Kindness, Oh God

How precious!
How infinitely precious
is Your smiling love, Your loving warmth
O Divine Judge Who is also within me
That I, child of man, take sheltered refuge within You
And from Your bounty, I take sustenance
And from Your pleasant waters, I drink deeply
Because only with You
is the fountain of my living waters
is the eternal spring of my life
is the source of my life
is the sense and meaning of my life
Because only in Your light do we see the light
Only in love and kindness, grace and goodness,
mercy and justice, compassion and solicitude,
trust and understanding and faith
can we see the light
Only in all life and in all living can we see the light
Only in living within You can we see the light
Only in living within Your law
can we see the light
Only in the atmosphere of God can we see the light
O God, only in Your love, can we see the light
Let Your smiling love pour down upon those of us
who would know You - O Lord
O Divine Judge Who is also within me
Let my loving warmth flow up
and merge with that smiling love
So that I would be
upright, steadfast, and straightforward
How precious!
How infinitely precious
is Your smiling love, Your loving warmth
O Divine Judge

Leon Leigh Faden

My Favorite Family Haggadah

A Fun, Interactive Passover Service
For Children & Their Families

Written by Shari Faden Donahue
Illustrated by David Aronson

ARIMAX, INC.

FOREWORD

As an intermarried Jewish woman, I have worked enthusiastically to keep Judaism flourishing - both in and out of the home - for our two young daughters, Maxime and Ariele. Though my husband, Tom, has not converted from his Christian faith, he has encouraged and supported our Judaism to such a degree that the three of us affectionately refer to him as our "Jewish helper."

Participation in the great wealth of Jewish holidays throughout the year has provided for our family a strong sense of Jewish identity, tradition, and values. Of all the Jewish holidays, Passover surely ranks as one of our favorites!

It is a time when we celebrate the joy of life, the dignity of freedom, and the ability to worship as we choose - in the tradition of our relatives who lived before us. As we immerse ourselves in Jewish history at our Seders, year after year, we find that valuable lessons emerge. In the presence of those dearest to us, we vow that ALL human indignities shall forever cease - regardless of an individual's faith, creed, or color.

It is unfortunate that many valuable lessons may be missed at a Seder too abstract or long-winded to comprehend. Thoughtless, spiritless repetition in ritual often breeds a lack of understanding for our great Jewish culture. It is with this in mind that *My Favorite Family Haggadah* has been created.

My Favorite Family Haggadah presents an exciting, thought-provoking 20 to 30-minute service designed especially for children and their families. Through captivating pictures, action, and song, participants shall journey enthusiastically through the inspirational story of Passover. Both young and old alike shall be uplifted by a strong sense of pride in their rich Jewish heritage as they revel in the miraculous, unbroken existence of the Jewish people.

SETTING THE CEREMONIAL SEDER TABLE

- Large circular plate or *Seder plate* with the following:
    - (1) Roasted lamb shank bone
    - (2) Roasted egg
    - (3) Fresh parsley
    - (4) Fresh bitter herbs such as horseradish root, radish, or leaf of romaine lettuce *(grows bitter when permitted to remain in soil for extended period)*
    - (5) Charoset - Blend 2 c. peeled, chopped apples, 1 c. chopped walnuts or pecans, 1/4 c. sweet red wine or grape juice, 3 Tbsp. honey, 2 tsp. cinnamon
- Candles for the blessing
- Wine, juice or non-alcoholic sparkling beverage for the blessing
- Salt water for dipping *(pass family-style for ceremony)*
- Prepared red horseradish
- Matzah plate with 3 matzahs and matzah cover
- Extra matzah
- Elijah's cup filled with wine *(place on center of table)*
- Small dish at *each* place setting with the following *(As an alternative, these ceremonial foods may be passed family-style)*:
    - slice of fresh horseradish root, radish, or leaf of romaine lettuce
    - sprig of fresh parsley
    - charoset *(recipe above)*
    - hard boiled egg *(shell removed)*
- Pillow for the chair of the host and/or hostess

POINTERS FOR A SUCCESSFUL SEDER

- Seder host or hostess begins Seder by reading first page of service *(page 7)*, which includes leading blessings over candles and wine.
- Next, in clockwise direction around Seder table, participants take turns reading individual paragraphs until service is completed.
- ALL participants "rap"*(speak rhythmically)* or sing Haggadah songs *in unison.*
- Be prepared with *afikomen* prize *(such as gelt, small toy, sweet treat, etc.)* for every child at conclusion of Seder.
- If time and attention permit, encourage discussion about the story of Passover as it relates to current events and world struggles.

PASSOVER SERVICE

Welcome to our Passover Seder. Here, we celebrate the joy of life, the dignity of freedom, and the ability to worship as we choose - in the tradition of our relatives who lived before us. Let us nurture our future as we learn from our past. Join us in our journey as we study the story of Passover, and grow from the strength of our ancestors.

We begin by lighting and blessing the holiday candles.

בָּרוּךְ אַתָּה יְיָ, אֱלֹהֵינוּ מֶלֶךְ הָעוֹלָם, אֲשֶׁר קִדְּשָׁנוּ בְּמִצְוֹתָיו וְצִוָּנוּ לְהַדְלִיק נֵר שֶׁל יוֹם טוֹב.

Baruch Atah Adonai, Eloheinu Melech ha'olam, asher kidshanu b'mitzvotav vitzivanu lehadlik ner shel Yom Tov.

בָּרוּךְ אַתָּה יְיָ, אֱלֹהֵינוּ מֶלֶךְ הָעוֹלָם, שֶׁהֶחֱיָנוּ וְקִיְּמָנוּ וְהִגִּיעָנוּ לַזְּמַן הַזֶּה.

Baruch Atah Adonai, Eloheinu Melech ha'olam, shehecheyanu v'keyimanu v'higianu lazman hazeh.

We praise You, O Lord our God, for granting us life, for commanding us to kindle these festival lights, and for bringing us together to share this happy occasion.

Next we sing the kiddush, the blessing over the wine - the traditional symbol of joy.

בָּרוּךְ אַתָּה יְיָ, אֱלֹהֵינוּ מֶלֶךְ הָעוֹלָם, בּוֹרֵא פְּרִי הַגָּפֶן.

Baruch Atah Adonai, Eloheinu Melech ha'olam, boray peri hagafen.

We praise You, O Lord our God, for the sweet grapes that grow to make the wine for our special holiday celebration.

Passover is a very special holiday which helps us to remember how lucky we are to be free. A long, long time ago, before we were born - even before our parents were born, the Jewish people were slaves in a faraway land called Egypt. Children, just like the children at this table, were not allowed to play, or sing, or skip, or live in nice houses, or eat any of their favorite foods.

They had to work very hard all day and all night with their moms and dads building palaces and cities for a wicked king. His name was Pharaoh, and he hated anyone who was Jewish. He shouted at them in a big mean voice ("RAP" [speak rhythmically] OR SING IN UNISON):

Bang...Bang...Bang...   *Dig...Dig...Dig...*
Hold your hammer low!   *Get your shovel deep!*
Bang...Bang...Bang...   *Dig...Dig...Dig...*
Give a heavy blow!   *There's no time to sleep!*

For it's work, work, work,
Every day and every night,
For it's work, work, work,
When it's dark and when it's light.

Pharaoh was especially mean to Jewish children. He did not want them to grow up to become moms and dads. He did not want the Jewish people to become strong. One Jewish mom was so afraid that she hid her baby in a basket which she had woven out of some tall weeds growing by the Nile River. To keep him safe, she floated the basket down the

river to where Pharaoh's daughter, the princess, was swimming. The princess was filled with joy when she saw the beautiful Jewish baby, and brought him home to the palace with her. She made him a prince, and named him Moses. In Hebrew, Moses means "pulled from the water." The princess kept the secret that Moses was a Jew.

The years passed, and Moses grew into a man. He watched, in horror, as the Jewish slaves were brutally whipped and beaten. Moses could not bear for the Jewish children and their families to be treated so cruelly. He jumped to the aid of one terribly weak slave and defended him with all his might against the evil Egyptian task masters.

The secret was discovered by ALL that Moses was not a true Egyptian, but the Hebrew son of slaves. Fearing for his life, Moses fled across the desert and made his home in the faraway land of Midian. There, Moses lived in a tent instead of a palace, however, he was happier than he had ever been in Egypt. He married a woman named Zipporah and worked for her father, Jethro, taking care of sheep. Moses and Zipporah had two sons.

One day, Moses was watching Jethro's sheep on the top of Mount Sinai. His eyes came upon a burning bush - a green, healthy bush which miraculously was not being harmed, even slightly, by the

raging fire. Moses then heard a voice calling to him from inside the bush. It was the voice of God. God told Moses to return to Egypt and help the Jewish children and their families right away. God turned Moses's shepherd's stick into a snake, then back into a stick again.

Moses understood the true power of God. He returned to Egypt to see the new Pharaoh as God had instructed him. The Pharaoh, more wicked than all others who had lived before him, was sitting high on his exquisite throne made of sparkling, shimmering jewels. Moses said ("RAP" OR SING IN UNISON):

Oh listen...Oh listen...
Oh listen, King Pharaoh...
Oh listen...Oh listen...
Please let my people go...
They work so hard all day...
They want to go away...
King Pharaoh, King Pharaoh...
What do you say?

King Pharaoh was angry. He shouted in a big, mean voice ("RAP" OR SING IN UNISON, AND POUND ON TABLE FOR EFFECT):

No! No! No! I will not let them go!
No! No! No! I will not let them go!

King Pharaoh looked Moses straight in the eye and laughed, "Ha ha ha... I will never let your Jewish people go. The Jewish slaves will do as I tell them, and will build grand palaces and cities for me just as I command." Moses replied, "If you do not free the Jewish children and their parents immediately, you shall be punished!" The wicked Pharaoh only laughed louder and shouted, "I am not afraid of you or your God - the God of the Jewish slaves. I shall be punished by no one!"

But God did punish Pharaoh because he was so wicked to the Jewish people. One of God's punishments was to make zillions of frogs jump everywhere - ooh! Let's "rap" or sing together:

One morning, King Pharaoh woke in his bed...
There were frogs in his bed and frogs in his head...
Frogs on his nose and frogs on his toes...
Frogs here...frogs there...
Frogs were jumping everywhere!

God decided to punish Pharaoh in ten different ways. These punishments are called *The Ten Plagues*. With the little finger, let's place a drop of wine on each of our plates, as we name them. The drops of wine remind us of drops of blood. We feel badly when people suffer, even when they've been unkind to us.

1) Blood	*6) Boils*
2) Frogs	*7) Hail*
3) Lice	*8) Locusts*
4) Wild beasts	*9) Darkness*
5) Cattle disease	*10) Death of first-born son*

Let's sing about the plagues to the tune of *The Ants Go Marching One By One* (or *Johnny Comes Marching Home*):

God made Pharaoh's water turn to blood...to blood
Hail crashed upon his head with a thud...a thud
Frogs were jumping everywhere
Lice got tangled in his hair
And locusts filled the land and the air (buzz buzz buzz)

The cattle started getting sick and died...and died
Blackness filled the days - no one could hide...could hide
Boils popped out on his face
Beasts roared all over the place
And first-born sons were killed without a trace

At last, Pharaoh became truly frightened of the powerful God of the Jews. He wanted the plagues to stop. He told Moses to take his Jewish people out of Egypt right away. The Jewish children and their families had to hurry. They were afraid that Pharaoh would change his mind and force them to stay in Egypt as slaves.

Moses and his people took all of their belongings - their clothes... their cows... their sheep. They also took dough to have bread to eat for the next day, but they did not have time to let the dough rise or bake. Instead they carried the raw dough on their backs. The sun was so hot that it turned the dough into matzah, just like the matzah we have on our table tonight (*hold up piece of matzah for all to see*).

All of the Jewish children and grown-ups followed Moses out of Egypt. Let's stand up by our seats and march in place as we, too, pretend to be hungry slaves leaving Egypt carrying our heavy belongings. (*Let's make comments about the make-believe desert we're walking through; how hungry, thirsty, and tired we feel; how heavy our belongings are; etc.*) Now, let's sit down.

Meanwhile, Pharaoh's queen taunted him for being humiliated by his own Jewish slaves. Pharaoh grew angrier and angrier, and sent his swiftest chariot army to recapture them. Let's stamp our feet to sound like Pharaoh's strong army chasing the Jewish children and grown-ups.

The Jewish children and grown-ups ran as quickly as they could from Pharaoh's army. When they reached the Red Sea, they panicked because they could go no further without drowning. God told Moses to lift up his shepherd's stick and stretch out his hand over the sea. Like magic, the sea opened, forming two miraculous walls of water with a path of dry land for the Jewish children and grown-ups to run safely across. Pharaoh's army followed them, getting closer and closer and closer. Once every Jewish child and grown-up made it safely off the path to the other side of the sea, Moses raised his shepherd's stick once again. Instantaneously, the sea fell mightily upon Pharaoh's soldiers and drowned them all.

Finally, the Jews were free! Oh, how happy the Jewish children and their families were! The children sang cheerful songs with their moms and dads and shouted, "Hooray for Moses!" Moses instructed the Jewish children to celebrate Passover each and every year - and when they grow up, to teach their children how special a privilege it is to be free!

Like our Jewish relatives of so long ago, we, too, are thankful for many wonderful things. Let's take a few minutes for each person here tonight to share why he or she is especially thankful (*family, health, freedom, etc.*). Now, let's sing a song of freedom and independence to the tune of *Havah Negilah* or recite as a poem:

*We have begun our Seder
with candles burning ever so bright.
Our strength shall not waiver
by the warm glow of their glimmering light.*

*I want to grow up strong...
And learn right from wrong...
I want to be the very best I can be!*

*Working hard night and day...
No time for sleep or play...
Is not the kind of life I choose for me!*

Free-dom! Free-dom! Free-dom!

*Let us relive our story...
Tell it in all its glory...*

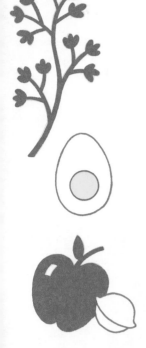

*It'll be our gain...
Remembering the pain...
To nev-er have slav-er-y a-gain!*

See Music
Page 31

To help us remember that we were not always free, we make our Seder table very different from our regular dinner table. There is a Seder plate with special foods on it (*point to each item as it's mentioned*): **charoset**, **bitter herbs**, **shank bone**, **parsley**, and **roasted egg**. Can everyone see them?

- *Charoset*, made with apples and nuts, looks like the mortar or cement used by the Jewish slaves to build Pharaoh's cities and palaces.

- *Bitter herbs* help us to remember the bitter lives of the Jewish children and their families when they were forced to be slaves in Egypt. (*Examples of bitter herbs are horseradish root, radish, or even romaine lettuce for it grows bitter when permitted to remain in the soil for an extended period.*)

- *Shank bone* from a lamb is symbolic of the power of God to protect all of those who believe in him. It also represents the very first Passover celebration when the Jews roasted a lamb and ate it with matzah.

- *Parsley* represents springtime when the sun shines, trees sprout new green leaves, flowers bloom, and the Passover celebration begins.

- *Roasted egg* reminds us of new life - a new beginning for the Jewish people.

As we tell the story of Passover each and every year, it is customary for us to sing the *The Four Questions* in Hebrew.

THE FOUR QUESTIONS

מַה נִּשְׁתַּנָּה הַלַּיְלָה הַזֶּה מִכָּל הַלֵּילוֹת?

Ma nishtanah halailah hazeh mikol halaylot?

שֶׁבְּכָל הַלֵּילוֹת אָנוּ אוֹכְלִין חָמֵץ וּמַצָּה. הַלַּיְלָה הַזֶּה כֻּלּוֹ מַצָּה.

Shebechol halaylot anu oaklin chametz u'matzah. Halailah hazeh kulo matzah.

שֶׁבְּכָל הַלֵּילוֹת אָנוּ אוֹכְלִין שְׁאָר יְרָקוֹת. הַלַּיְלָה הַזֶּה מָרוֹר.

Shebechol halaylot anu oaklin sh'ar yerakot. Halailah hazeh maror.

שֶׁבְּכָל הַלֵּילוֹת אֵין אָנוּ מַטְבִּילִין אֲפִילוּ פַּעַם אֶחָת. הַלַּיְלָה הַזֶּה שְׁתֵּי פְעָמִים.

Shebechol halaylot ain anu matbilin afilu pa'am echat. Halailah hazeh sh'tay f'ahmim.

שֶׁבְּכָל הַלֵּילוֹת אָנוּ אוֹכְלִין בֵּין יוֹשְׁבִין וּבֵין מְסֻבִּין. הַלַּיְלָה הַזֶּה כֻּלָּנוּ מְסֻבִּין.

Shebechol halaylot anu oaklin bayn yoshvin u'vayn misubin. Halailah hazeh kulanu misubin.

Now that we've sung *The Four Questions*, let's answer them in English to be sure that we understand the true meaning of Passover.

Why is this night different from all other nights?

On all other nights we eat all kinds of breads and crackers. Why do we eat only matzah on Passover?

Matzah helps us to remember that the Jewish children and their parents left Egypt in a hurry. The sun baked the dough which they carried on their backs into hard crackers called matzah.

There are three matzahs on our special matzah plate (*point*). The three matzahs represent the three groups of Jews who lived in ancient Israel during the days of the temple: Kohanim (*the high priests*), Levites (*those who served the high priests*), and Israelites (*all others*). (*All Jewish people are descendants of one of these groups.*)

We break the middle matzah into two pieces. We place one of those pieces, called the *afikomen* (*Greek word for dessert*), inside a matzah cover or napkin, and hide it. (*Adult briefly leaves the table to hide the afikomen.*) At the end of our Seder meal, all of the children here tonight will have the opportunity to find the *afikomen* (*no peeking allowed*) and win a prize.

The Jewish children and parents of long ago could not make it through the desert without matzah to sustain them. Symbolically, we cannot conclude our Seder this evening without the children finding the *afikomen*. When the *afikomen* is found, we will break it into small pieces and share it for dessert.

Now, let's each take a small piece of matzah. We make two blessings over the matzah, and then eat it:

בָּרוּךְ אַתָּה יְיָ, אֱלֹהֵינוּ מֶלֶךְ הָעוֹלָם, הַמּוֹצִיא לֶחֶם מִן הָאָרֶץ.

Baruch Atah Adonai, Eloheinu Melech ha'olam, hamotzi lechem min ha'aretz.

We praise You, O Lord Our God, for bringing forth bread from the earth.

בָּרוּךְ אַתָּה יְיָ, אֱלֹהֵינוּ מֶלֶךְ הָעוֹלָם, אֲשֶׁר קִדְּשָׁנוּ בְּמִצְוֹתָיו וְצִוָּנוּ עַל אֲכִילַת מַצָּה.

Baruch Atah Adonai, Eloheinu Melech ha'olam, asher kidshanu b'mitzvotav vitzivanu al achilat matzah.

We praise You, O Lord Our God, for giving us Your special commandments and for the matzah which reminds us of how we fled from Egypt.

On all other nights we eat many kinds of herbs. Why do we eat bitter herbs called "maror" on this night?

Bitter herbs help us to remember the bitter, miserable lives of the Jewish children and grown-ups who were slaves for the wicked Pharaoh. Let's make a sandwich of two small pieces of matzah and some bitter herbs. As we eat it, let's groan and pretend that we, too, are slaves in Egypt.

On all other nights, we usually do not dip herbs. Why, at our Seder, do we dip two different herbs?

First, we dip fresh bitter herbs (*slice of fresh horseradish root, radish, or leaf of romaine lettuce*) into charoset so that we can remember how terribly hard the Jewish children and grown-ups worked building the cities and palaces of ancient Egypt. Before we eat it, we make a blessing:

בָּרוּךְ אַתָּה יְיָ, אֱלֹהֵינוּ מֶלֶךְ הָעוֹלָם, אֲשֶׁר קִדְּשָׁנוּ בְּמִצְוֹתָיו וְצִוָּנוּ עַל אֲכִילַת מָרוֹר.

Baruch Atah Adonai, Eloheinu Melech ha'olam, asher kidshanu b'mitzvotav vitzivanu al achilat maror.

We praise You, O Lord Our God, for the bitter herbs to remind us of the bitter slavery we endured.

Next, we dip parsley into salt water. We pretend that the salt water is the tears of all the Jewish children and grown-ups who cried because of the wicked Pharaoh. Before we eat it, we make a blessing:

בָּרוּךְ אַתָּה יְיָ, אֱלֹהֵינוּ מֶלֶךְ הָעוֹלָם, בּוֹרֵא פְּרִי הָאֲדָמָה.

Baruch Atah Adonai, Eloheinu Melech ha'olam, boray peri ha-ah-damah.

We praise You, O Lord Our God, for the herbs and vegetables that grow.

On all other nights, we eat any way we choose. Why, on this night, do we eat in an especially comfortable position?

The evil Egyptian task masters forced the Jewish children and their families to stand as they gulped tiny portions of tasteless food. Tonight, at our special Passover Seder, we celebrate our freedom from slavery. We sit proudly and comfortably at our beautiful Seder table, and enjoy many delicious foods in a relaxed and leisurely manner. As a symbol of our comfort and well-being, the host and/or hostess leans on a pillow throughout the Seder meal. (*In ancient days, people who enjoyed freedom and status ate their meals while reclining on pillows.*)

The egg in front of each of us is a symbol of life and fertility. It also represents a new beginning for the Jewish people. Let's now eat our egg.

Let's sing a song of thanks for the freedom of all the Jewish people from Egypt.

Dai-yenu

Ilu hotzi, hotzianu,
Hotzianu miMitzrayim,
MiMitzrayim hotzianu,
Dai-yenu.

Dai-dai-yenu,
Dai-dai-yenu,
Dai-dai-yenu,
Dai-yenu, dai-yenu!

Ilu natan, natan lanu,
Natan lanu et ha Torah,
Natan lanu et ha Torah,
Dai-yenu.

Dai-dai-yenu,
Dai-dai-yenu,
Dai-dai-yenu,
Dai-yenu, dai-yenu!

On this very special Seder night, we are expecting a very special Seder guest. In fact, let's open the door for him (*open the door*). Can anyone guess who this special guest is? Yes. His name is Elijah, and we have a special cup of wine for him on our table (*point*). This is the cup of Elijah. Elijah was a great and kind teacher, or prophet, who lived many, many years ago. He was always helpful and loving to those around him, and the Jewish children and their parents were grateful to him and loved him in return. Many Jewish people believe that Prophet Elijah will visit our Seder to tell us of the coming of the Messiah - the miraculous One who will come to us when the time is right to make ALL that is bad or painful or scary or sad disappear like magic!

As we open the door to Elijah, we watch his cup to see if any of the wine disappears. If he arrives tonight (*just maybe he will!*), we sing a beautiful chorus which was created especially for him so that he knows he is welcome.

Eliahu hanavi,
Eliahu hatishbi,
Eliahu, Eliahu,
Eliahu hagiladi.

Passover is a celebration of freedom - freedom to worship as we please, freedom to be ourselves, freedom to be the best human beings we can be. As we relive our exodus from Egypt during our unique Seder ritual, we are reminded, over and over again, that freedom is a privilege which we must *never* take for granted!

Even today, in many parts of our world, children and their families are treated unfairly as the Jewish people have been throughout history. We strive for the day when every man, woman, and child can live in peace, dignity, and freedom.

Each of us here tonight must work to make our world a better place. By valuing and protecting the rights of ALL humankind, we will make the difference. As we patiently await Elijah's visit, "We must be the change that we wish for the world."

Now, let us raise our glasses and toast,

"To life...L'CHAIM!"

BUILDING CITIES

Bang, Bang, Bang, hold your ham - mer low.
Dig, Dig, Dig, get your sho - vel deep.

Bang, Bang, Bang, give a hea - vy blow. For it's work, work, work, ev - 'ry
Dig, Dig, Dig, there's no time to sleep.

day and ev - 'ry night. For it's work, work, work, when it's dark and when it's light.

LISTEN KING PHARAOH

Oh lis - ten, oh lis - ten, oh lis - ten, King Phar - aoh. Oh lis - ten oh

lis - ten, please let my peo - ple go. They want to go a - way. They

work too hard all day. King Phar - aoh, King Phar - aoh, what do you say?

No, no, no, I will not let them go.

ONE MORNING

One morn - ing when Phar - aoh woke in his bed, there were

frogs in his bed, and frogs on his head, frogs on his nose and frogs on his toes,

frogs here, frogs there, frogs were jump - ing ev - 'ry - where.

FREEDOM

We have be-gun our Se - der with can-dles

burn - ing ———————————— ev - er so-o bright

Our strength sh - all not waiv - er by —— the

warm glow of —— their glim - mer ing light

I want to grow up strong And lea - rn right from wrong I want to

be the very best I - can be Work - ing hard night and day

No time for sleep or play is not the kind of life I cho - ose for

me Free - dom Free - dom Free - dom

Let —— us re - live our stor - y Tell —— it in all its glor - y

It'll be our gain Remembering the pain To never have slav - er - y a - gain.

My Favorite Family Haggadah

is dedicated to

my favorite "Jewish helper"- my husband, Tom,

who has empowered me

with his openness, sensitivity, and love...

our daughters,

our two most precious gems,

Maxime & Ariele...

and our one and only Bubbie Bec.

ARIMAX, Inc.
Post Office Box 53
Washington Crossing, PA 18977
Phone: (215) 862-5899
Fax: (215) 862-9720
E-Mail: arimax1@aol.com

Design: David Stencler & Michael Butler
Technical Assistant: Thomas W. Donahue
Editor: Rochelle (Shelley) Faden
Rabbinical Consultant: Rabbi Elliot J. Holin
Consultants: Bec Faden, Marci Shander, Risa & David Rudick, Steve Freedman, Ellen Tilman

Library of Congress Catalog Card Number: 93-74503

ISBN 0-9634287-1-3

First printing, 1994
Second printing, 1996
Third printing, 1998
Printed in the United States of America

How Precious Your Loving Kindness, Oh God (second page) is an original composition by my father, Leon Leigh Faden. This "love song to God" emerged from the prayer, *Ma Yakor*, chanted during the highly sacred ritual of enveloping oneself in one's tallit - an act of supreme devotion to God.

A note of appreciation to Shirley Cohen for her words/music to the following songs: *Building Cities, Listen, King Pharaoh*, and *One Morning* (Record: *Passover Music Box*, © 1951 by Kinor Records)

"We are the change that we wish for the world" (page 28) - quote by Mahatma Ghandi